Faithbuilders Publishing

A Benediction of Bluebells

T0349775

by Doreen Harrison

A Benediction of Bluebells by Doreen Harrison

First Published in Great Britain in 2019

FAITHBUILDERS Ltd

Bethany, 7 Park View, Freeholdland Road
Pontnewynydd, PONTYPOOL NP4 8LP
www.faithbuilders.org.uk

British Library Cataloguing-in-Publication Data

A catalogue record for this book is available from the British Library

ISBN: 978-1-913181-14-7

Cover Design by Faithbuilders

Cover Image © Gemphotography | Dreamstime Stock Photos.

Other stock photo illustrations used under license from Dreamstime and are credited throughout.

Printed and bound in Great Britain by Marston Book Services Limited, Oxfordshire.

By the same author: Fragrance of Faith, A Bouquet of Blessings, A Garland of Grace, Daffodils in Winter, The Donkey Boy, Jubilant Jeremy Johnson, Coping with the Wobbles of Life.

These books fit into an A5 envelope, each one makes a delightful birthday gift, get-well gift, or a gift for any occasion! The books can be read as daily meditations and in subject, cover the entire year.

Contents

I dedicate this book to my grandchildren – Max, who is training to be a doctor, Rachel, who is training to be a nurse, and who inspired the story on page 36 entitled "The Power of Touch," and Lotte, who is in 6th form and concerned, like me, that we will always have bluebells in spring, and continue to maintain the quality of life on planet Earth.

Bluebells

We live in a beautiful valley. I look outside and consider the contour of our mountains, the quantity of wooded areas, and the jubilant cascade of the river. And in spring, I love to see the bluebells! Bluebells appeared in the UK after the last ice age, and half the world's bluebells grow in the UK's ancient woodlands. Native British bluebells have Spanish cousins, which have no scent and are paler in colour. These were introduced in the Victorian age as a garden plant. Now they grow in the wild; and crossbreed with the native flower.

British bluebells are a protected species, and if you dig up a bluebell plant, you could incur a fine of up to £5000! After all, it takes five years for a bluebell seed to grow into a bulb, and if bluebell leaves are crushed (i.e. trodden on) the plant will die for lack of food, because the leaves can no longer photosynthesize.

In the middle ages, feathers on arrows were stuck in place with glue made from bluebells, and during the reign of Queen Elizabeth I, starch made from crushed bluebell bulbs was used to regenerate big ruff collars. Bluebells are poisonous. They contain 15 biologically active compounds to defend the plant against animal and insect pests. Scientists are now researching how these toxic chemicals might be used to cure cancer. So don't miss the bluebells! Unfortunately, they are included in the million (or more!) species now at risk of extinction.

After a weeklong meeting in Paris, experts from 50 countries issued a warning that, "a mass extinction event, precipitated by human activities, is already underway." Many species of birds, beasts, bees, butterflies, and bluebells will vanish. The £1.8 million report states, "Humanity must take action NOW." Robert Watson, chair of the group that drafted the report, said, "The loss of species, eco-systems and generic diversity is already a global and generational threat to human well-being."

So – don't miss the bluebells; enjoy them while we still have them! This spring, our woods are sweet with these lovely flowers. I thank God for the privilege of living in a rural area, and pray for wisdom and care as the nations of the world struggle to maintain the quality of life here on planet earth. I pray, earnestly, the first words of the prayer which Jesus taught us:

> "Our Father in heaven, hallowed be your name, your kingdom come, your will be done, on earth as it is in heaven." (Matthew 6:9–10)

Image © Ocskay Bence

To the End of Our Lives

> *"Do not cast me away when I am old; do not forsake me when my strength is gone. Even when I am old and grey, do not forsake me, my God, till I declare your power to the next generation, your mighty acts to all who are to come." (Psalm 71:9, 18)*

There comes a time when another birthday inclines us to cling with gratitude to Bible promises such as these verses from Psalm 71! The way we are to do this is found in verses 6 and 7 of the same psalm:

> *"I will ever praise you. … My mouth is filled with your praise, declaring your splendour all day long."*

It is a tremendous opportunity for witness, when we become "old and grey" in the Lord's service. Consider this explanation of my statement: The prevailing problem with the children of

Israel, on their journey from Egypt to the promised land is that they grumbled! Having crossed the Red Sea on dry land they sung with gusto, *"In your unfailing love you will lead the people you have redeemed, in your strength you will guide them to your holy dwelling!"* This is reported in Exodus chapter 15:13. Yet in verse 24 of the same chapter we read, *"So the people grumbled!"*

Exodus chapter 16 verse 2 begins, *"The whole community grumbled."* Exodus chapter 17 verse 3 continues the sad story: *"and they grumbled."* The saga continued, and unfortunately continues, for humanity is extremely prone to grumble!

Which is where our opportunity comes in. To count our blessings and rejoice in the Lord is to become a sign and witness to many that Jesus saves, keeps, and satisfies – right to the very end of our lives. Now, I can write this because I am "old and grey" – although "mature" may be a more comfortable adjective to accompany the colour of my hair! I am not preaching at you: I am promising you, based on my own experience, that Jesus always keeps his word, and *He will be with you* – even to the very end of your life.

When kind people ask you how you are, just remind them of your own faith, and simply say, "Ah! God is good!"

Image © Ljupco

One Hundred Not Out!

I enjoyed reading the account of a lady who reached her 100th birthday and received the anticipated greeting card from the Queen. She said, "I expected the card to be bigger than it was!" To have been alive for 100 years is certainly an achievement which deserves maximum notice. Life is a gift and we should celebrate its continuation.

People are living longer these days; in fact, the Queen has had to take on more staff to ensure that every 100th birthday is remembered!

I recollect an item about an insurance agent who was trying to persuade a pensioner to take out extra security for the next ten years. The old man replied, "Son, at my age I don't even buy green bananas!" Statistics can rise or fall, but the only absolute certainty for any of us, is that one day our life will come to an end. This is as certain as the adamant fact that night follows day – and, equally, that day follows night.

Yet the Christian faith declares that death is not the end. The Bible explains that, *"For God so loved the world that he gave his one and only Son, that whoever believes in him shall not perish but have eternal life" (John 3:16).*

When I was a teenager, someone asked me to visit a certain old lady called Mrs. Honey, to cheer her up! She was as sweet as her name, and the cheerful encouragement came from her to me! Her wisdom, and experience of patience in affliction taught me more than any lecturer or college course could do. One day, I was explaining about my holiday plans – where I would go, how I would get there, what I would wear. She listened, with a smile. When I had finished, she said, "My dear, let me tell you, in one sentence, about my marvelous holiday plans. One day, soon, I will be on my way to Heaven!"

In our society, such a comment could be dismissed as "Bananas!" It may be that we have allowed our faith to become old and grey, when God is offering us His joy, His presence, His future. In spite of old age, it can be continual springtime in our soul.

Cold Turkey!

Three dramatic stories! First event. Invitations had been sent, preparations made, all was ready to greet the new year in style. About midnight, the prize turkey was placed in the oven, to cook at a very low heat all through the night. When the day of the celebration came, the main course was disappointing – they had forgotten to switch the oven on, and the turkey was still cold and raw!

Second drama! The contracts had been exchanged, a date fixed for the new owners to move in, and with an hour to go before they arrived, they took a last look around the house which had been a happy home for so many years. And then, disaster! There was no water! Every tap ran dry! They made a frantic call to an emergency plumber, who said "maybe" he could come. This was followed by an earnest call to the new owners, whose furniture van was already en route to their new home. They gave a final twist to the tap in the kitchen, and then remembered that they had turned the water off following a final check on the heating system!

Third episode. The dear old lady regarded her stair lift as a priority. She went up and down on it each day, and eventually (as she became extremely frail and wobbly), even put on the seat belt! And, then, unexpectedly, the stair lift stopped working! She crept upstairs, on her hands and knees. However, on reaching the top, she realised what had happened. She had switched the power off, by mistake!

These three events all have one thing in common. On each occasion, there had been no power. Now, a question for you – have you checked your power supply? Friends, family, future, frailty, whatever, however, and forever, the Bible gives this advice:

> *"Commit your way to the Lord; trust in him and he will do this: he will make your righteous reward shine like the dawn, your vindication like the noonday sun. Hope in the Lord and keep his way. He will exalt you to inherit the land; when the wicked are destroyed, you will see it. The salvation of the righteous comes from the Lord; he is their stronghold in time of trouble." (Psalm 37:5, 34, 38)*

How is your power supply? Are you switched on to the never-failing supply of energy, grace, and goodness of God's resources?

Something to Sing About

Consider this poem:

> "Special moments, are they large ones? Big with presence,
> pomp and show?
> Every day brings special moments, small things, that give life its
> glow.
> Shopping precinct, rush and bustle, pavement café – custom
> slow –
> Rain is falling, maybe most folk think it best to buy and go!
> One small girl is sitting there, and, all at once, she starts to sing.
> Childish voice, in Welsh, her solo turns the winter into spring!"

Think about the verse for a moment. It is a cold, wet day, grey and dull. A day to get the shopping and then get home. One little girl begins to sing. What does she sing? Does it matter? She thinks she has something to sing about, and so she does.

It is so easy to miss the special blessings which, "turn winter into spring." If it rains, fix your umbrella, and look for the rainbows! If company and conversation are restricted because most folk have no time – or get too busy to take time to be companionable – tomorrow might be different. There will always be another day, however dark the night.

Listen, look and lighten today: an old hymn advises, "Count your blessings, name them one by one." If you have read this so far, you have already identified that you can see, you are educated, and you can read what you like. No one points a gun at you, you live in a free country, the planes flying overhead do not carry bombs. If you had been amongst the number of people who thought it best to "buy and go!" you have had money to spend, in shops with full shelves, and you have a home to return to.

And if you are hard of hearing and could not hear the child sing, we are blessed with the NHS, who will provide you with a hearing aid.

We live in a Christian country, where people worship a great God, who loves them. The Bible assures us that:

> *"God is our refuge and strength, an ever-present help in trouble. Therefore we will not fear, though the earth give way and the mountains fall into the heart of the sea." (Psalm 46:1–2)*

Now, that would be, "a large moment, big with presence, pomp and show!" But every day, God is with us – and surely that is something to sing about?

Image © Michael Ahanov

Brussels Sprouts

Our grandchildren cooperated in the production of a very special present, which has already provided laughter and pleasure through many dark days. They wrote, "Memories of grandad and grandma," 52 of them, on individual slips of paper, and put them in a jar, labelled, "Pick one a week." This is the one we picked at the beginning of February. It is written by Rachel.

"When I was little, (and also older!) I made sure I sat by grandad at Christmas dinner, so he could eat my Brussels sprouts!"

During the Brexit campaign a few years ago, we heard continuous predictions concerning the possible results of Brexit – empty shelves, no fresh fruit or vegetables – and so I wondered if my granddaughter had a political reason for saying, "No more sprouts from Brussels, please!"

Our Brexit actions will no doubt affect us UK citizens, but they will also affect other countries in Europe. The situation merits careful consideration of the Biblical admonition, *"Love your neighbour as yourself."* We should be aware of the future and well-being of other ordinary Europeans, like us, who are eager for peace and prosperity.

In the well-used simile of the glass half full and half empty, I detect a kind of pessimism in society which provokes the question: "Why have some thrown the glass away altogether?"

There are many reasons for optimism. Outside I see the signs of Spring – snowdrops, daffodils, and a profusion of early blooms lining the roadside. Catkins are already shaking their pollen lengths in the wintery wind. It is possible to read, even without the light on, at 5.00 pm!

So winter has come and gone, and spring has arrived. During the process of Brexit, and in future political changes, we must trust our Government, trust the inbred common sense of the British public, but above all – trust God. He never makes a mistake.

Panic or Prayer?

How unnerved we are! In early 2019, the thought of a possible drone flight over a runway at Heathrow airport led to all flights being suspended. "Get the headlines as they happen," suggested the BBC News. Was this another way of saying, "Prepare to panic?" "The authorities are taking this incredibly seriously!" proclaimed the announcer. In our advanced society, it's amazing that a few lights in the twilight sky can provoke such an incredible reaction. The reporter continued, and I quote: "Is this an alarming, sinister attempt to close our major airport?" Fear! Alarm! Panic! What had happened to all our wishes for a Happy New Year?

These days, when we listen to a news broadcast, what if we put a tick for what is positive, and a cross for what is negative?

Probably before we were halfway through, we would see that the crosses will outnumber the ticks!

I recollect an incident in the life of a missionary lady, Gladys Aylward – known as the small woman, because she was! Many years ago, she led a group of 100+ children over the mountains in China, to the Yellow River, on the other side of which was safety from the Japanese army. But with war so near, panic prevailed and there were no boats to take them across. For four days, Gladys and the children waited, hungry, and tired, but not in despair. Gladys gathered the children around her, and they would sing and pray. She knew the situation was hopeless. She realised that there were no boats. She admitted to herself that she had no power to open the vast waters of the Yellow River. But God could, and so she continued to pray that He would.

There was a platoon of Chinese Nationalist soldiers, scouting on this (wrong) side of the river. The officer in charge was suddenly aware of an unexpected sound. It was children! Children, singing. Cautiously he mounted a slight rise in the bank above the river – and saw them, Gladys and her 100 children on the beach, singing! And he was able to summon boats across to carry the weary tribe to safety! No panic, just prayer and praise and patient faith in God who never fails to provide for us if we allow Him to do so. Panic is unproductive. Prayer promotes peace. The Bible states:

> "Commit your way to the Lord; trust in him...." (Psalm 37:5)

He cannot fail, for He IS God.

The Month of February

In view of the uncertainties of the future, I find it reassuring to consider the month of February and identify some positive facts. It's a short month with 28 days clear, and 29 in each leap year. It is a cold, dark, wintery month, yes – but you can always depend on its shortness! Thus, it presents a worthy lesson for living.

Dark, dismal days do not last forever. We celebrate in verse: "February brings the rain – thaws the frozen lake again." February is something temporary!

At the bottom of the steps to our house, where we keep the dustbins, there are snowdrops. We did not plant them, they just appeared one spring, and every year they survive and blossom, as if to reassure us that when winter comes – spring will always follow. February is a reassuring month. Miserable, maybe, but in buds, shoots, early flowers, catkins, flirting birds, and longer days it is mightily eloquent. It reminds us that, *"As long as the earth endures, seedtime and harvest, cold and heat, summer and winter, day and night will never cease" (Gen 8:22).* In other words, we can expect things to improve. A wintertime of dustbins has not diminished our doughty patch of snowdrops.

This morning, as I sat in our GP's waiting room, redolent with wheezes and sneezes, on the receptionist's desk there was a vase of daffodils, a silent message: "Cheer up! Things can only get better!"

There is wise advice in the Bible. Consider these words: *"I urge, then, first of all, that petitions, prayers, intercessions and thanksgiving be made for all people, for kings and all those in authority, that we may live peaceful and quiet lives in all godliness and holiness."(1 Timothy 2:1–2)*

I appreciate these words by John Updike. "The days are dark – the sun's a spark – hung thin between the dark and dark. The sky is low – the wind is grey. The radiator purrs all day." Now that is optimism. The radiator continues to purr. No power cut! Look for what IS happening, not what might happen. Not disaster, not defeat. This is the day God has given you – make it a perfect day, by trusting him to bless you, guide you and guard you. And he will.

Image © Olesia Teteria

Cherry Blossom

In the northern hemisphere, spring begins on March 20th and makes way for summer on the 21st of June. The astronomical calendar determines the seasons, due to the 23.5 degree tilt of the Earth's rotational axis in relation to its orbit around the sun. In spring, Earth's axis is tilted towards the sun, and the vernal equinox presents 12 hours of day light and 12 hours of darkness.

Spring is the season of rebirth. Pablo Neruda wrote: "You can cut all the flowers, but you cannot keep spring from coming!" Shakespeare identifies, "Proud pied April dressed in all his trim hath put a spirit of youth in everything." Spring is absolutely inevitable! The Bible promises, "As long as the earth endures, seedtime and harvest, cold and heat, summer and winter, day and night will never end." Notice that this inclusive promise begins with seedtime – spring. Here in our town, we have a lovely park, which is just beginning to awaken after a winter sleep. The cherry trees will bud and blossom with a beauty which achieves national celebration in Japan! In fields around the town, lambs skip and play. In gardens and allotments, seeds begin to push through the softening soil, and our emblem flower, the daffodil, dances in gardens, along roadsides, on verges beside the motorway. Birds sing, squirrels forage for forgotten supplies of hidden nuts, and magnolia blossoms dominate many gardens, high and lifted up on a sunny day, with flamboyant loveliness.

"Hope springs eternal in the human breast," said Alexander Pope, whose dictum is still as profound as it is poetic! Hope is the belief one holds during difficult circumstances, that things will get better. Of course, they will. God is in ultimate control of the affairs of humankind. And Gods timing is as perfect as that of the predictable next vernal equinox.

Now, consider these words from the Bible:

> *"Praise the LORD. Give thanks to the LORD, for he is good; his love endures for ever." (Psalm 106:1)*

Image © Anujavijay

Hot Cross Buns

Hot cross buns! Traditionally eaten on Good Friday in Great Britain, Ireland, Australia, Canada and some parts of the Americas (according to Wikipedia!) A sweet, spiced bun made with currants and raisins, and marked with a cross on top. Progress has also caught up with bakers — and now, toffee, orange and cranberry, apple and cinnamon, coffee, cherry and chocolate, and butterscotch flavoured hot cross buns are available all the year round!

Hot cross buns originated in the UK, and they mark the end of Lent, when restrictions on certain foods are lifted. A monk, Brother Thomas Radcliffe, from St. Albans, introduced the spicey bun with a cross on top, in honour of Good Friday, in 1361, and distributed them to the poor on that day.

In 1592, Queen Elizabeth I issued a decree forbidding the sale of hot cross buns except on Good Friday or at Christmas! Of course, hot cross buns are now available throughout the year. Legends accrue: It is said that if you hang a hot cross bun from your kitchen roof on Good Friday, it will remain fresh and mould free for the rest of the year, just as the body of Jesus, who called himself the Bread of Life, had no sign of decay after his crucifixion and prior to his resurrection.

In 2014, an Australian baker had the novel idea of producing a NOT cross bun, decorated with a smiling face! A Bible reference for this version would be, *"The joy of the LORD is your strength" (Nehemiah 8:10),* and an appropriate name could be, "the hallelujah bun."

It is theologically accurate to present hot cross buns all through the year. Christ is not just for Easter. Good Friday was not an end, but a beginning. Jesus rose from the dead, as he said he would. He will never break his promise to be with us, always, even to the end of time! So, the classic Easter hymn, "Jesus Christ is risen today, Hallelujah!" is suitable for every day.

As another old hymn declares, "New every morning is his love, our wakening and uprising prove. From sleep and darkness, safely brought, restored to life, and power, and thought."

Image © Orientaly

Daisies on a Roundabout

If you were to visit my home town at the moment, you would notice the amazing proliferation of daisies on local roundabouts. Years ago, an award winning sculptor, Robert Kennedy, worked with 360 young students from local comprehensive schools to create a series of sculptures called Beacon, Dreamboats and Tower, which were placed on local roundabouts. The variety and originality of these sculptures has provoked much comment over the years, but perhaps the daisies really deserve a headline of commendation!

Spring is prolific with floral tributes to God who has created all things well. Consider Wisteria – it's always a joy to behold. The grim old walls of our local prison are festooned with their sweet-scented purple sprays. May blossom, hawthorn, abounds. Hedgerows are already rich with buttercups, cow parsley, and ragged robin. And the grass this year seems to possess a new vibrancy of green colour! So many common place enhancements in our little valley, which often go unnoticed.

There is one thing we can be sure of whenever days are dark and dreary – there will always be another springtime! Ralph Emerson proclaimed, "The earth laughs in flowers." And a lady with the last word, Anne Broadstreet, wrote, "If we had no winter, the spring would not be so pleasant!"

But the Bible says it best of all, (of course)! God promises, *"As long as the earth endures, seedtime and harvest, cold and heat, summer and winter, day and night will never cease" (Genesis 8:22).* Nor have they. Nor will they. However, take note of the word "endures." Recent news reports have identified a limit to the number of years this old planet can continue. Pollution, over population, greed, selfish political decisions which disregard human needs and safety make "endure" an apt word to describe the way the Earth must cope with the way humanity has mistreated it.

And, yet, the daisies continue to beautify our roundabout. Maybe a timely reminder that our sophisticated society needs to regain an awareness of the simple things of life.

Sandwiches

On an occasion in 1762, the 4th Earl of Sandwich, who was an inveterate gambler and did not want to leave his game of cards, ordered his valet to bring him some portable food, easy to eat, and satisfying. His cook obliged with meat, tucked between two slices of bread. Others noted this easy meal, and began to order, "the same as Sandwich!"

We have become avid sandwich samplers, wherever, and whatever they contain. Over the Easter weekend last year, I experienced two very different sandwich meals. One contained a large amount of coronation chicken, salad, roasted garlic, and mayonnaise – and the bread matched the contents of the sandwich in size! It was served on a wooden platter, and when I cut it, the delicious contents erupted out of the bread. The other sandwich was very different. Wafer thin, crusts cut off, filled with slices of cucumber, and served on a dainty china plate, it was a delectable resume of a Sunday tea from decades ago. One thing that both had in common, however, was that the main ingredient for each sandwich was bread. In the sandwich, bread is the factor which holds everything together.

I am certain that neither the Earl of Sandwich, nor his cook, intended to produce a parable for abundant living when that first sandwich was made – but that is actually what can be identified! Whatever, however, whoever, wherever, whenever – Jesus, who describes himself as the bread of life, holds everyone and everything together.

Modern life is filled up with so many different things. My 23-year-old grandson, a fourth year medical student, announced over an Easter meal, "Things have changed so much in my life time, I can't keep up with them!" Like those two amazingly different sandwiches, life offers so much variety – but the bread of life has not changed. Jesus, the bread of life, is the way the truth, and the life. Without his surrounding grace, we fall apart. His final promise, in St Matthew's Gospel, states:

> *"And surely I am with you always, to the very end of the age." (Matthew 28:20)*

However you fill the sandwich of your life, the presence, power and peace of Jesus can and will hold you together – always.

Image © Murburger01

The Spider Web

What an amazing world we live in! For instance, next time you undertake the mundane task of dusting away a spider web in the corner of the kitchen window, consider the material with which it is constructed!

Spider silk is light, thin, and five times as strong as steel. The problem of producing spider silk in industrial quantities seems to have been solved by a manufacturer in Japan, who has worked with insect genetics researchers from Shinshu university to produce a new type of silk thread by incorporating spider genes into silkworm eggs! Sericulture, or silkworm farming, is an important cottage industry in Japan. Silkworms, hatched from these eggs, produce thread which is 10 per cent spider thread, and which is used for a variety of textiles and other products, such as sutures for surgery, fishing lines, and body armour for troops! Maybe the spider web in the corner of your window is on a par with the largest suit of armour in any Medieval castle, so far as protection and strength are concerned!

I heard a news reader on the radio commenting that the hot weather has caused fruit to ripen and rot. Wasps, who live on the sugar produced by rotting fruit, are intoxicated by the alcohol content in the fermenting fruit. So are the wasps in August buzzing or hiccupping? Whatever, the spider web in your kitchen is strong enough to catch the most drunken wasp in its flight towards you!

Now, in the kaleidoscope of experiences, events, expressions, and excitements of everyday life, we can miss out on the real adventure of being alive because we are always looking ahead for the major events, and thus miss out on the minor marvels! We are like inebriated wasps caught in the steel trap of the little spider's web! Consider the simple chorus of an old hymn:

"All things bright and beautiful, all creatures great and small. All things wise and wonderful, the Lord God made them all!"

Whoever, however, wherever you are today, you are living in a wonderful world, created by the Great Designer, God. The Bible declares, *"I remain confident of this: I will see the goodness of the Lord in the land of the living." (Psalm 27:13)*

Image © Sergii Koval

Yorkshire Pudding

The other day, I came across the word used locally for spring onions – "jibbons." The word apparently comes from the south-west of England, although in Welsh, it is "sibwns," a word which is taken directly from Norman-French, "chiboule" (onion), a word which has been in use since the 1500s! Language is local, but it moves from locality to locality, just as we do. Maybe Shakespeare had this in mind, when he wrote, "What's in a name? A rose by any other name would smell as sweet!"

I was a rotund teenager, probably as a result of a diet of Yorkshire pudding preceding the main course. We always had Yorkshire pudding first, to reduce our appetite for main course meat, which was expensive. We also had it for pudding (hence its name!) filled with sultanas and sprinkled with sugar. Hence my ample waistline! I remember spending some time in Northumberland, and being frequently introduced as, "Our bonny friend from Yorkshire." I appreciated this: in Yorkshire, "bonny" means "attractive." Then I discovered that in Northumberland, it meant "tubby." My appreciation diminished.

Dialect words are fascinating – how they originated, and how we use them. A new neighbor of ours, eager to come to terms with her different surroundings, went to get the local paper. She was on her way out of the shop when the assistant pointed out that in spite of the paper's name, "The Free Press," she needed to pay for the paper! The word "free" in this context is not a reference to the price, but to the fact that the paper is not restricted by people or politics, but intends that, as E. C. Cummings once wrote: "The truth will emerge from free discussion!"

So – what's in a name?

Consider this verse, from the Bible. Joseph was assured about Mary: *"She will give birth to a son, and you are to give him the name Jesus, because he will save his people from their sins." (Matthew 1:21)*

The name Jesus means "Saviour."

Language may change from place to place, but the Bible affirms that, *"Jesus Christ is the same yesterday and today and for ever" (Hebrews 13:8),* and declares, *"I, the Lord, do not change" (Malachi 3:6).* We are also told, *"Salvation is found in no one else, for there is no other name under heaven given to mankind by which we must be saved" (Acts 4:12).*

Having begun this article with thoughts of food, I now conclude it with food for thought! Bon appetite, my friend!

The Power of Touch

My enthusiastic granddaughter belongs to a group of young people who visit a residential home for old people, many of whom have dementia. "What do you do there?" I asked. "I gently stroke their hands," she replied! I read recently in "Psychology Today" that touch is the first sense we acquire, and so it is the secret weapon in any successful relationship! Just holding their hands probably helped these dear old people to feel valued and appreciated. With this thought in mind, I read with some amazement another article about Japan. Having stated that Japan is a virtual robot kingdom, the writer informs us that if you grow old in Japan, you can expect meals to be served by a robot, expect to ride in a voice recognition wheelchair, and even expect care from a nurse in a robotic suit!

At a home care convention in Tokyo, a spoon-feeding robot with a swiveling arm helped elderly people eat their food. These are accepted as ways to cope with a greying population. But old people are special! They are the product of their enterprise, energy, durability, purpose, determination, and prayer. Their past has created our present. As their physical presentation decreases, we must never diminish them by assuming that emotionally and spiritually they can no longer understand what is happening around them. They need instead to feel accepted and loved. They warrant the comfortable touch of friendly fingers.

I am reminded of a former young pupil of mine who specialized in getting everything wrong! I took him by the hand to lead him to the arithmetic corner for necessary catching up, when he suddenly said, "Miss, my little hand feels so safe with you holding it!" A most unexpected result for that teaching episode, and one which taught me that people of any age need to feel cared for. Can robots really fill that role? Should society, legislation of health and safety, or other people's opinions be allowed to negate the affirmation of touch?

A moving instance in the life story of Jesus describes how he reached out and touched a leper. The Christian faith features a God who came in person to hold our hand. He offers to guide us and encourage us. Consider these words from the Bible, where God said, *"My hand will sustain him; surely my arm will strengthen him." (Psalm 89:21)*

Image © Kevin Carden

The Lost Sheep

There is a story about a shepherd who had 100 sheep and lost one of them. The account tells us that he left the 99 sheep and looked for that lost sheep – which he eventually found. So, what was special about that sheep? How valuable was it? A Google search informed me that the most valuable sheep in the world was bought for £251,000 in 2009. That's a real Ferrari in the flock! However, there is no value ascribed to the sheep in our story; it was just one amongst many, and it got lost. Maybe it was old, and unable to keep up with the rest, or maybe this sheep forgot where it was! (I wonder, do sheep have memory to lose?)

We are inclined to embroider the facts of the story, to give this sheep attributes which it did not possess! Perhaps it just couldn't keep up with the march of time! To the shepherd, this poor old sheep was as important as the rest, and he set off to look for it. One old sheep!

The media regale us with dire predictions concerning an elderly population. Can the country afford to look after so many pensioners? We can cope with active old people – it's the "lost" ones we find difficult. Those who are inactive, due to arthritis or stroke; those who are inarticulate, due to diseases such as dementia; those who are frightened by their inability to understand modern ways of living (you have to be smart to use a smart phone!); those who are lonely or poverty stricken; and all those who, for a variety of reasons, have lost the joy of living.

The story of the lost sheep is in the Bible. God is the shepherd, and He sent Jesus to seek and to save the lost. In our present preoccupation with the problems faced by young people, please remember older citizens who lose out because they seem to be less useful, or uninteresting. Perhaps they themselves have lost interest in the world around them. Consider these words:

> "I will praise the Lord all my life; I will sing praise to my God as long as I live." (Psalm 146:2)

He remains faithful forever!

Image © Igor Stevanovic

A Time of Crisis

It is easier and more comfortable to blame someone else when things go wrong. Often, if we were more honest, we would realise that many of the problems which plague our everyday lives are exaggerated by our reaction to them!

A crisis is not helped by the public alarm which erupts when desperate decisions have been made by those in power. Possibly the need is for public concern for those who bear responsibility for the future prosperity and peace of the people whom they represent. A potential can of worms might even become caterpillars and turn into butterflies!

I am a little old lady, a retired primary school teacher. I learned to approach this primary age group realistically when I discovered that even the smallest eleven-year-old could look me in the eye! But I had authority – I was in charge – and a riot of 200+ pupils would quit when I took command and said (albeit loudly), "Stop it at once!" I took my example from Gladys Aylward, a small lady missionary in China many years ago, who once stood in a prison yard, with rioting convicts all around. Taking authority, she shouted, "Stop it at once!" And they did! So – what was her authority? Before she addressed the mob and faced the danger, she reminded herself of this verse in the Bible:

> *"I can do all this through him who gives me strength."*
> *(Philippians 4:13)*

These words are not a mantra of faith: they are an affirmation of fact. If God is for us, who indeed can be against us? God's influence in society seems to be reduced to small letters – in fact, "god" is no longer included in most of our public decisions. Our Father in Heaven is not compelled by creed or surprised by conduct. He is concerned with love for all the nations of the world. And, amazingly, He trusts us with His authority to say, "Stop it!" when violence and evil, and mistaken reactions and beliefs erupt in society.

Consider this advice, written 2000 years ago but very applicable today:

> *"I urge, then, first of all, that petitions, prayers, intercession and thanksgiving be made for all people – for kings and all those in authority, that we may live peaceful and quiet lives in all godliness and holiness." (1 Timothy 2:1–3)*

Indeed, this is good advice!

Image © Zhanghaobeibei

Banana Extinction

We can become quite blasé when confronted with dire headlines proclaiming the demise of yet another natural species. After all, this is an age of scientific expansion, and when we read that there are only two white rhinos alive in the world – both female – we can readily comprehend the importance of the possibility of creating a test-tube embryo, using frozen sperm from a dead white rhino male, in order to save the threatened species!

But recent headlines have provoked more personal agitation. Consider this: "Bananas threatened with extinction!"

Now, this is extinction in our own fruit bowl! Written references to bananas date back to 500 BC. Here in the UK, we consume 5 billion bananas in one year. Half of human DNA is also owned by a banana! And now, yellow bananas are threatened by a fungus disease called "fusarium," which attacks the root system, and for which, at the moment, there is no defence.

There are 1,200 types of banana on planet earth, but the fungal disease is no respecter of species. In this lovely summer season, we applaud the promise which God made to Noah, *"As long as the earth endures, seedtime and harvest, cold and heat, summer and winter, day and night will never cease." (Genesis 8:22)*

Maybe we need to concentrate on the opening phrase, "As long as the earth endures?" With the frequently quoted adage in mind: "Elderly people don't buy green bananas!" should we consider the wisdom of "going green" as our social responsibility? When God finished His creation we read that He saw all that He had made, and it was very good. It is vital that we begin to reassess our care and concern for the amazing gift of planet Earth. We are each responsible for our own small corner; the possible demise of the yellow banana is a warning light before the final red light stops all movement!

Against this dark background – enjoy these words from Psalm 100:

> *"Shout for joy to the Lord, all the earth. Worship the Lord with gladness; come before him with joyful songs. … Enter his gates with thanksgiving and his courts with praise; give thanks to him and praise his name. For the Lord is good and his love endures for ever; his faithfulness continues through all generations." (Psalm 100:1–2, 4–5)*

Bananas might disappear, but God is everlasting!

Potato Crisps

I saw an amazing sight in our local supermarket! I stood at the end of a long aisle, and noticed that on all the shelves, on both sides, from top to bottom, were bags of potato crisps made by many different manufacturers, all in different shapes, sizes, prices, and flavours. Yet all these were derived from the same source – the potato. And I was amazed that our consumer society actually considered such a variety to be an economic proposition.

But maybe for not much longer. The recent summer heat wave has taken its toll on farms and allotments. Potatoes, carrots, and all root vegetables, struggle; without grass, dairy farmers are already feeding their herds with next winters hay. Whatever is the world coming to?

I saw a dire report in a national newspaper which declared: "Earths overshoot day arrives early." It explains that the world has hit the day on which we have used all the resources the planet provides for the rest of the year! And with the collection of crisps still fresh in mind, I noted that this report also advises that it would take three Earths to sustain the world if everyone lived like we do in the UK.

Some crops delight in this high degree weather. Grapes thrive, lemons ripen, olives are in their element. But wheat, barley, and other grain crops are severely affected. The prolonged heat wave of last summer devastated crops across Europe. Farmers were anxious about the impact of the heat wave was having on both crops and livestock. But where can we go from here?

There was an event in the life of Jesus when a large crowd – more than five thousand – were hungry. His disciples asked, "How can we feed all this lot?" Jesus asked what food was available, and they produced five loaves and two fish! Jesus took the food, prayed and then gave the disciples a continual supply with which they fed the crowd, the Bible affirming that, *"They all ate and were satisfied." (Matthew 14:20)*

Consider this advice from the Bible:

> *"Trust in the Lord with all your heart and lean not on your own understanding; in all your ways submit to him, and he will make your paths straight." (Proverbs 3:5–6)*

Pray for provision for all the population of planet Earth. You can depend on Gods care and concern. That's very crisp advice!

Image © Andrew Vernon

The Flower Show

I remember my first visit to the Chelsea Flower Show. Perhaps surprisingly, my abiding memory is not of the incredible displays in the Pavilion, the amazing collection of speciality gardens, the glorious roses, the lupins (taller than me), or even the business of the bees in their Chelsea heaven. No, my delight was a display of violets on a corner stand, not included in the list of medal winners. Quietly presenting their own loveliness, it was undoubtedly true that small is beautiful.

Mother Theresa wrote, "Be faithful in small things, because it is in them that your strength lies." We may not be able to do great things, but we can do small things in a great way!

Consider this well-known story from the Bible. David, who killed the giant Goliath, was small in his family's eyes. When Samuel the prophet was prompted by God to visit his family home to anoint the future king of Israel, David was not included in the group. He was looking after the sheep. And even in those days, that was not an important job. One of his brothers declared later, "With whom did you leave those few sheep in the wilderness?"

But David did his small work well. As he told giant Goliath, who sneered at his size, *"You come against me with sword and spear and javelin, but I come against you in the name of the Lord Almighty, ... the battle is the Lord's." (1 Samuel 17:45–47)*

I always try to appreciate the ordinary things of life. They represent the few sheep in our wilderness. Keep your eyes and mind and soul and strength fixed on the Lord God Almighty. With Chelsea in mind, remember that a rose is honoured for its beauty, not its size. It is not the size of the seed which is important, but the size of what grows from it. We don't judge a tree by its size, but by its fruit. If you feel that your personality and position in society are violet size, don't waste your precious gift of life by longing to be bigger, better, bolder, or more beautiful. Take advice from the Bible. Learn to be content whatever the circumstances, and identify with this truth, *"I can do all this through him who gives me strength." (Philippians 4:13)*

Picking Strawberries

Here's a thought for summer. Nowadays, supermarkets sell strawberries all the year round, but these imported fruits do not have the same "zing" as our British strawberries!

That word, "zing," is an accurate way of describing the action of a freshly picked strawberry on our taste buds! I have a sweet memory of a June day, in Kent, when we collected our two small daughters from school and went to the strawberry farm to pick our own fruit. We were in an area of chalk, so we were picking crimson berries, which nestled amongst green leaves, with sun-bleached white soil and a clear blue sky. Sky larks were singing overhead. This memory encompasses all our senses. Touch – the firmness and warmth of the dimpled fruit. Taste – of sweet strawberries. Smell – of sunbaked, chalky soil. Sight – of the white ground, the red fruit, the green leaves, and the sun bright sky. Hearing – the sky larks and the happy voices of fruit pickers. So many reasons to thank the Lord, for He is good.

Amongst the strewn debris of broken promises, an insecure future, and unhappy political alliances, we must take time to be grateful for what we have. Take time to praise God for all the good things which your five senses can discern and remind yourself that He has indeed done all things well.

Make your witness personal. Stating, *"I know that my Redeemer lives," (Job 19:25)* is as positive an experience as picking juicy strawberries on a sunny day in June! So start each day by reminding yourself:

> *"The Lord has done it this very day; let us rejoice today and be glad." (Psalm 118:24)*

Let this be your daily intention, wherever, whatever, and however you are. And may God bless you, real good.

rowing Older

It's July! We are halfway through the year and the school year will soon end. Parents will be concerned as to which school, college, or university their children will attend next year.

An ancient philosopher declared, "Time is a game played beautifully – by children!" As we grow older, we agree more with other explanations about time, such as "time flies! No time left! Running out of time! Time and tide wait for no man!" The habits, intentions, and decisions of everyday life change as new aspects of time alter our lifestyle.

A recent survey of pensioners asked participants to give alternatives to the title "elderly." Choices included, "senior citizen," "retired person," "grey panther," and even "silver surfer!" I quite like the term "silver surfer!" However steep, however high the waves of circumstance, however fiercely they curve over us, faith in God will keep us buoyant and ready for the next swell in the tide of life.

Old age is inevitable. It is the culmination of all the excitement, suspense, variety, sweetness, trauma, drama, pain, and pleasure of being alive. Napoleon is reputed to have said, "There is one kind of robber whom the law does not strike at, and who steals what is most precious to me. I refer to Time." When time is full of distress, disease, disappointment or despair, do not allow these thieves to steal your peace! Cling to God's presence.

Consider these words:

> *"As for me, I shall always have hope; I will praise you more and more. My mouth will tell of your righteous deeds, of your saving acts all day long – though I know not how to relate them all. I will come and proclaim your mighty acts, Sovereign Lord; I will proclaim your righteous deeds, yours alone. Since my youth, God, you have taught me, and to this day I declare your marvellous deeds. Even when I am old and grey, do not forsake me, my God, till I declare your power to the next generation, your mighty acts to all who are to come."* (Psalm 71:14–18)

God promises to be with us always. His promises never fail. He has always kept me in His care. I know who holds my future. How about you?

Image © Elena Elisseeva

Rainbows of Blessing

I was arranging the display of work for parents' evening at the Infants School where I was working. Stories, carefully written, pictures, pages of arithmetic, accurate and neat. Every child was included – except Mario. He was tall for his age, always kind and helpful, but reading, writing and arithmetic were not on his agenda in class! Finally I found a small picture, recognisable as a face, under which he had labouriously printed. "This is my Mum." I mounted this on rainbow coloured card and added it to the display. Came the evening, parents, grandparents, inquisitive older siblings and pupils arrived. I noticed an excited group with Mario, and I went to greet them. Mario's Mum took my hand. "I am so proud," she said, "my son's work is on the wall. Thankyou for all you have done for him!" So what had I done? I had accepted Mario as he was and cared that he felt accepted and encouraged. I chose to identify what he could do, rather than home in on what he couldn't do.

I remembered this incident as I watched the news just the other day. Attention was focused on a ship, crowded with immigrants, which had been turned away from Italy and Malta, meaning that the people on board were facing a further voyage to Spain. There were children board, too, whose perception would be, "Nobody wants us. Nobody cares!" A little boat drew alongside, and the crew handed up boxes of red, juicy fruit – a rainbow of refreshment from concerned people.

I thought, too, about Noah and his family. When they all came out of the ark, after months of darkness – and the smell of all those assorted animals – what might they have expected? What happened was that God placed a rainbow in the sky, an encouraging reminder of His love and care. It is Gods pleasure to present rainbows of blessing on our darkest days. His most amazing rainbow of hope was when Jesus rose from the darkness of death. Consider this promise from the Bible:

> "For as in Adam all die, so in Christ all will be made alive." (1 Corinthians 15:22)

A poet wrote, "I trace the rainbow through the rain, and know the promise is not vain, that morn shall tearless be."

Image © Robert Kneschke

The Scooter

As we sat in the sunshine, enjoying the beauty of this summer weather, three young children were playing nearby. One of them had a cute little scooter, and the other two watched him as he carefully scooted around. The next child pushed the scooter along. Then the older child told him to stand on the scooter and use one leg to propel himself onwards.

The third child, who was a toddler, watched them intently. When they moved away, leaving the scooter, he toddled across, and rolled the wheels. Then he lifted the scooter and put one leg on it. The scooter slid to the ground and he fell off. But undeterred and unhurt, he got up, got on again and this time, got going! I was only half way through my cup of coffee, and he had learned the art of riding a scooter.

Children learn by imitation. They watch what we do. They identify our words and copy them. Our habits become their habits. They adopt the pattern of the world around them so quickly that it is becoming imperative that somehow social media, television, and smartphone apps, are monitored for the sake of our children's propensity to copy what they see and hear. Also, we ourselves need to be mindful that we are audible and visible to young eyes and ears all the time.

In the scooter episode, child number two did as he was instructed. But the third child learned by imitation. In this season of summer shows and fairs, and in markets and super stores, you can enjoy free samples of all sorts of things. We are, by our actions, reactions and words, free samples of behaviour and personality! So, what sort of example should we present in today's complex society?

The Bible suggests:

> *"But the fruit of the Spirit is love, joy, peace, forbearance, kindness, goodness, faithfulness, gentleness and self-control. Against such things there is no law. ... Let us not become conceited, provoking and envying each other." (Galatians 5:22–23, 26)*

Image © Boobathy

The Colour of Love

Amongst the debates, discussions, deliberations and denials concerning the creation of the world, the one undeniable proof, for me, is that the world is full of colour! It is bright and beautiful, admirable and amazing. We are approaching the season of autumn, when green leaves turn amber, ochre, saffron, copper, bronze, and rust. Twilight skies are often a delicate shade of green. When Noah and his family came out of the ark, we read that God curved a rainbow over them as a sign of His love. Maybe He presented His love in every colour of that rainbow to reassure them that whatever happened next, He would bring light into each emotion and need.

We use colour to describe emotions. When everything is going well, we declare that we are "in the pink!" When things do not work out as we expected, we feel "blue." We describe being "green with envy," or "red with rage." We call cowards "yellow." Special events are "purple patches!" The ultimate accolade is to be "as good as gold."

However, when we speak of "black depression," we indicate that the light has gone out of our lives. The good news is that God specialises in bringing light into our darkness. There is an old prayer that affirms this truth: "Lighten our darkness, we beseech thee, O Lord, and by thy great mercy, defend us from all perils and darkness of this night." And He certainly will, when we ask Him to do so.

In light, every colour of the rainbow is held in perfect balance. Light does not contain black. Black is the absence of light. Faith switches on the light of the knowledge of the glory of God in the face of Jesus Christ. He is the light of the world.

In my classroom, we were arranging a collage of autumn pictures. When it was gloriously finished, and we were admiring the combination of colours: lemon, primrose, mustard yellows, crimson, scarlet, ruby reds, navy, royal, kingfisher blues, emerald, lime, and pea greens. I asked the children, "And which do you like best?" Noel (renowned for naughtiness!) spoke up first, "Them poisonous toad stools, Miss!" Undaunted, I asked, "Why?" With surprise, he replied, "The colour is so beautiful!" In our drab, doleful, and often dangerous world, look out for the colour of God's love.

Succulent September

Succulent September is an appropriate description of this autumn month of harvest in the hedgerows. Blackberries abound! Who can resist the clusters of juicy, sweet fruit, just waiting to be picked and enjoyed?

In the late 19th century, when whooping cough was prevalent in England, it was common to pass small children through the bramble bush as a cure. Once through the bush, an offering of bread was left under the arch in the belief that the disease would leave with the food.

In our enlightened age of medical science, people do not take these superstitions seriously, and so you are no longer likely to see a slice of bread under a bramble bush. Yet, unfortunately, the Lord Jesus who is not a superstition but *the bread of life*, is seldom petitioned when we are ill.

So when we reach another September, and you see the splendour of the brambles in full fruit, pray for our nation. Progress in every aspect of life has carefully, clearly, callously, cunningly removed any appetite for the bread of life.

Enjoy these Bible verses:

> *"Yet this I call to mind and therefore I have hope: Because of the Lord's great love we are not consumed, for his compassions never fail. They are new every morning; great is your faithfulness. I say to myself, 'The Lord is my portion; therefore I will wait for him.' The Lord is good to those whose hope is in him, to the one who seeks him; it is good to wait quietly for the salvation of the Lord." (Lamentations 3:21–26)*

Image © Lukas Gojda

Broken Strings

Yitzhak Perlman is a violinist of worldwide repute. An Israeli-American, he was born in 1945, but at the age of 12, he contracted polio, and now uses crutches and wears leg braces. He plays the violin sitting down. At a concert in New York, he was scheduled to play an extraordinarily challenging violin solo. A few seconds into his performance, one of his strings broke! The orchestra stopped playing. Usually, the violinist would have left the stage and quickly replaced the string. Perlman's disabilities made this an impractical solution – so he motioned the conductor to continue, and he played the piece, on three strings, with skill and beauty. When he finished, audience and orchestra rose to their feet, and there was tumultuous applause.

Perlman held up his hand for silence. He said, "All, my life it has been my mission to make music from that which remains."

How do you view October? Summer is past, the days are shorter, winter is almost with us. Emotionally, spiritually, do you ever anticipate a winter of discontent? In a small, maybe elderly fellowship, does modern society overwhelm you with its defiant dismissal of God and His purposes for planet Earth? Remember this fact. Winter is **ALWAYS** followed by Spring. The Bible suggests:

> "But one thing I do: forgetting what is behind and straining towards what is ahead, I press on towards the goal to win the prize for which God has called me heavenwards in Christ Jesus." (Philippians 3:13–14)

The musical score from which 10,000 times 10,000 will celebrate Jesus in Heaven includes your music and requires your melody.

A Prayer: Father in Heaven, you present us with the opportunity to glorify your name by the music of our living. Help us to make music by the way we represent your unfailing love and grace. Amen.

Be still,
and know
that I am Go[d]

Psalm 4[6]

In the Stillness

Summer has given way to autumn. Already Christmas is in evidence in the shops and on the TV and internet. Meteorology reveals what sort of weather we might expect this winter. It is October – a month between colour and celebration, coldness and a continuation towards spring. Consider this delightful description, written by Thoreau: "October is the month for painted leaves. As fruits, and leaves – and the day itself acquires a bright tint just before they fall, so does the year, near its setting. October is its sunset sky!"

This is a month when we can kick through the fallen leaves of hopes and fears, success and sadness, horrors and halfhearted hallelujahs, and clear the way for future blessings. Summer and winter are seasons of great contrast, and most of us have bittersweet experiences in life, whatever our creed might be.

Yet the changing seasons offer us a pause – space and time to be still and catch up.

The Bible expresses it like this:

> *"Be still, and know that I am God; I will be exalted among the nations, I will be exalted in the earth." (Psalm 46:1)*

Make October your opportunity to catch up on the spiritual side of life. We expend so much time and energy on the physical and emotional aspects and neglect the spiritual dimension. We can become so enmeshed in the amazing fact of being alive that we consider life immortal as fiction! Take time to think about God. Take time to explore the worship and praise expressed in your local church. Take time to express your hopes and fears to God. Ask Him to forgive you and take time to forgive yourself. Take time in October to be still in your soul.

Image © Motortion

Nylon Stockings

Back in the days when Woolworths was an indispensable asset to every shopping centre, I worked in a local branch as a "Saturday girl." One of my friends who worked with me was saving up for her wedding celebrations. Came the unfortunate day when the store manager made this announcement: "We will not pay you with money today. We have new NYLON STOCKINGS in store, and each of you will receive a pair of them!" My friend sighed. She said, "Well, I'll save them for my wedding." And she did!

Sometimes I try to count the incredible assortment of new items which have become available to buy since my Woolworth days! The speed of progress is incredible. The manager kept his word. We each received a pair of nylon stockings. Some of us can still remember garters and suspenders, can you? Those were the pre-tights days!

My friend got married and I am sure she is keeping her promise – "For richer or poorer, for better or worse, in sickness and in health, till death us do part." There was a time when we kept our promises. A time when our word was our bond. The saddest situation concerning Brexit in the UK is that promises have been broken, the Government is not observing the Referendum decision. As I write, there still seems to be no solution to the present impasse! Regarding my Woolworth experience, the offer of stockings instead of wages helped my friend, but I had an eye on my future college fees, so I looked forward to the next pay day in cash.

Things always get better! Woolworths is no more, but I have continued! Who knows what the future will be? But there will be a future, with changes and improvements!

Consider these words recorded in the Bible, and referring to God, the great Manager of the Universe:

> *"For the word of the Lord is right and true; he is faithful in all he does. The Lord loves righteousness and justice; the earth is full of his unfailing love. … For he spoke, and it came to be; he commanded, and it stood firm. … But the plans of the Lord stand firm for ever, the purposes of his heart through all generations." (Psalm 33:4–5, 9, 11)*

God will never let you down, He always keeps His promises.

November

Of all the months in the year, I always feel that November is the most nostalgic. Summer was special, with hot days and holidays, but autumn glows with superb colour – how delightfully creative of God to celebrate the entrance of winter with a palette of leaves, now ochre, bronze, rust, saffron, crimson, and copper! We review memories of commotions, concerts, capers, commiserations, companionship, congratulations, and with the celebration of Christmas clamouring for our attention, we wonder where the year has gone.

Well, now, once the juvenile jollification of November 5th is over, there is a pause in activity and we can take time to observe the advice in *Psalm 46:10, "Be still, and know that I am*

God; I will be exalted among the nations, I will be exalted in the earth."

Time seems to be in such short supply in our super-efficient society. We need space to catch up – to regain a composure of soul and a contentment of spirit. Turn off the TV, tune out the family, turn over your timetable, and just sit quietly by yourself. Then say, "Jesus, it's me," and you will discover that He is here, already, eager to meet you.

November can bring spring into your soul when you recollect that the joy of the Lord is your strength. In a medieval English hymn, Jesus has been described as "The Lord of the dance." Reach up to Him – and ENJOY being part of the family of God.

Wise Men United!

Is it only turkey and tinsel – carol singing and collections for charity – parties, presents, pantomimes – are these the elements which truly express peace on earth, goodwill to all people?

Christmas comes and goes. Another year begins and we move through another 12 months towards another celebration of the winter solstice. We can honestly ask, "Where is this peace and goodwill? It hasn't happened yet!"

Please consider the visit of three wise men on that first Christmas, 2000 years ago. They were obviously well equipped and made an impressive entrance into Jerusalem, because the Bible affirms, *"When king Herod heard the news he was disturbed, and all Jerusalem with him" (Matthew 2:3)*. This was no group of starstruck enthusiasts, with personal predictions to present. These were educated, affluent men who made a good impression on the officials – and they were in complete agreement about the purpose of their journey! This was a team, united together in their quest to find the King of the Jews. These were wise men, presumably well up on the historical background of the Jewish nation, and also believing that here was a way in which the entire world could experience peace – that through this Jewish Messiah would come goodwill towards all men, this was to be a universal king. They travelled together, they trusted each other, they followed the star of hope. They were a team, united in their quest.

When we hear our governments disabled by disputes and broken promises, and our country riven by doubts and fears, the following verse from the Bible offers a solution:

> "I urge, then, first of all, that petitions, prayers, intercession and thanksgiving be made for all people – for kings and all those in authority, that we may live peaceful and quiet lives in all godliness and holiness." (1 Timothy 2:1–2)

There is a very wise proverb which agrees with this solution:

> "Commit to the Lord whatever you do, and he will establish your plans." (Proverbs 16:3)

Why not try our Faithbuilders Bible Study Guides?

In this series so far: Matthew, Mark, Luke, John, 1 Corinthians, Galatians, Ephesians, 1 & 2 Peter, Esther, Amos, Hosea, Zechariah.

Read More from Doreen Harrison

A Bouquet of Blessings; A Garland of Grace; Fragrance of Faith; Daffodils in Winter

Coping with the Wobbles of Life

The Donkey Boy

Jubilant Jeremy Johnson

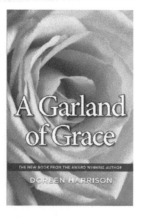
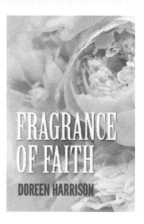